101
UNOFFICIAL
ROBLOX
STORY STARTERS

101 UNOFFICIAL ROBLOX STORY STARTERS

Get Kids Writing with Fun and Imaginative Video Game–Inspired Prompts

Sara Coleman

Published in the US by:
ULYSSES PRESS
PO Box 3440
Berkeley, CA 94703
www.ulyssespress.com

ISBN: 978-1-64604-136-7
Library of Congress Control Number: 2020946983

Printed in the United States by Bang Printing
10 9 8 7 6 5 4 3 2 1

Acquisitions editor: Claire Sielaff
Managing editor: Claire Chun
Project editor: Tyanni Niles
Editor: Renee Rutledge
Proofreader: Kathy Kaiser
Production: what!design @ what!web.com
Front cover design: Jake Flaherty
Cover artwork: plane © Golden Sikorka/shutterstock.com; roller coaster © BigMouse/shutterstock.com; fish © Macrovector/shutterstock.com; pizza © masmas/shutterstock.com; astronaut © Jake Flaherty

CONTENTS

INTRODUCTION

Welcome to *101 Unofficial* Roblox *Story Starters*, where your love for one of the world's most popular games meets a kickstart in creativity. Just as the game invited you to explore imaginary worlds of all kinds, this book is full of ideas to get the gears of your imagination turning. Whether you need help for a writing project in school or you want to write stories for fun, these story starters are designed to get your creative juices flowing.

Writers use story prompts all the time. It's a great way to inspire your next adventure through words. Will you write about something funny? Will you write about your favorite animals? You get to decide, and the result will be a story that is all yours and that no one can ever change but you!

HOW TO USE THIS BOOK

First, ask yourself what genre of story you would like to write. Are you looking for adventure or something along the lines of humor or horror? Perhaps you don't know what you're looking for quite yet, and you need a little inspiration to get you started. To begin your story, follow these steps:

* Locate the subject you're interested in within the table of contents.

* Once you find a subject, start brainstorming ideas about your character and setting.

* Start writing about what your character does, the events that happen to them along the way, and how your story might end.

* Introduce another character to your story if you think your character needs to meet someone else.

* Provide lots of details. What does your character look and sound like? What stands out about their location? Try to make the reader of your story feel like they are right there with you!

* Create an ending, and tie up any loose ends.

Remember, these are only starters and prompts. You can fill in the blanks in any way you want to. Change the character name, game, location, or any other details you would like to re-create. The beauty of your story is you are in complete control of what happens. You are limited only by your imagination.

ARE YOU STILL FEELING STUCK?

It's okay, we all need a little help sometimes. If you feel like you can't dream up any new ideas, all you need to do is ask yourself a few more questions. Soon, the plotlines and possibilities will multiply.

* What is my character thinking? Why is my character acting this way?

* What is my character doing throughout my story? What kind of action takes place to move the story along?

* What happens to my character or to the world that I've imagined? What does my character have to do to achieve their goals?

* What kind of ending does my story have? Does the ending resolve my character's conflict, or are there still questions left unanswered?

HOW TO FIND INSPIRATION WITHIN ROBLOX

Inspiration for your stories can be found anywhere! It doesn't take long to find something to spark your imagination, especially if you look at your favorite books or video games. Take the world of *Roblox*, for instance. Whether it's overcoming a pesky obstacle we refer to as an "obby" or making an adorable little digital friend we call a "meep," wherever you look, you can find a nugget to inspire your future story.

The game of *Roblox* is full of ideas you can use anytime you craft a story. Think about how many different games are within the world of *Roblox*, each created by someone who used their own ideas to invent it. *Roblox* takes it further by creating genres within the games, similar to how genres are used for books. Try experimenting with different genres and subgenres to make your own story.

Next time you're playing *Roblox*, notice how similar playing a game is to telling a story. First, you'll see where the game takes place—this is called the setting. Then, your character is introduced to the game and must now interact with the surroundings and other characters. And there is always some type of conflict in the world of *Roblox*! The game tells a story about life as a Robloxian, and now you can too.

How will your story begin?

CHAPTER 1

ADVENTURE

From high schools to the high seas, you'll find plenty of adventures throughout the games of *Roblox*. If you want to add a memorable experience to your own story, use these story prompts to get started.

If Gabriela could have one wish, it would be to fly—like the characters in *Royale High*. She would fly to another country and observe how other people live. She would even try a variety of international foods.

It's time to build a boat, just like in *Build a Boat for Treasure*. Kai designs the boat of his dreams and maps out where he wants to sail around the world. If only he could see the danger that lies ahead...

Addison was selected to be the shark in *Shark Bite*. She wonders where the sharks like to swim the most and what would happen if she had the chance to live among them.

_____

_____

_____

_____

_____

_____

_____

_____

_____

_____

_____

_____

_____

_____

_____

_____

_____

The Normal Elevator takes Jordyn to a new level. He doesn't know what will happen or what new world will be waiting for him there. Once he steps off the elevator and turns the corner, he soon sees why no one wants to stay on this floor.

Ava is sailing the boat she created. Everything is going smoothly until she hears a very strange noise coming from below deck. Something is clearly lurking down there, and the only way to find out what is there is to look for herself.

Collin needs a weapon to keep the shark from ripping his boat into shreds. It can't be any known weapon though—it must be a weapon the world has never seen before.

_____

_____

_____

_____

_____

_____

_____

_____

_____

_____

_____

_____

_____

_____

_____

_____

_____

Bree can't stop thinking about how rude the swarm of bees were to her. They chased her, tried to sting her, and then buzzed so loudly in her ear she couldn't think straight. Now she has a plan to chase them away so they will find a new home. And those bees will never see it coming.

_____

_____

_____

_____

_____

_____

_____

_____

_____

_____

_____

_____

_____

_____

_____

A potion is brewing, and it will be perfect for those living on the island. This potion is made of several liquids and seems to have special powers. It's going to be a huge help for the islanders, even if they have no idea what's in it!

_____

_____

_____

_____

_____

_____

_____

_____

_____

_____

_____

_____

_____

_____

_____

_____

Today is truly a bizarre day. The opposite of ordinary is happening, and nothing is as it's supposed to be. Something strange is going on and causing so much confusion.

Brynn was just selected as the beauty queen for her high school. While everyone is cheering her on, she wishes they knew who she really was. Would her friends still support her if they knew her secret identity?

_____

_____

_____

_____

_____

_____

_____

_____

_____

_____

_____

_____

_____

_____

_____

_____

The saga continues for Liz as she faces one obby after another. She's constantly working her way through the checkpoints to try to overcome them. But this obstacle is the absolute worst. She's never seen anything like it.

The bees are working together to escape from the bears. All the bears ever want is the bees' honey. The bees must outsmart the big, brown creatures, but what can they do?

_____

_____

_____

_____

_____

_____

_____

_____

_____

_____

_____

_____

_____

_____

_____

_____

_____

CHAPTER 2

TOWN AND CITY

It takes a lot of work to build a new city and then keep the town running. The Town and City games in *Roblox* are no exception. From city jails to dream neighborhoods, you can find tons of ideas within your own city block.

It's time to create your dream neighborhood in *Welcome to Bloxburg*. What do the houses look like? Who are your neighbors?

_____

_____

_____

_____

_____

_____

_____

_____

_____

_____

_____

_____

_____

_____

_____

Olivia is a cop in *Jailbreak* and must act fast to catch up with a criminal she spotted in town. She wonders how this criminal escaped from jail in the first place, and where the criminal plans to go next.

Lucas is curious about what it would be like to have a constant friend following him everywhere he goes, like a meep in *Meep City*. But where would Lucas and the meep go together? Where would the two end up?

_____

_____

_____

_____

_____

_____

_____

_____

_____

_____

_____

_____

_____

_____

_____

Charlie notices a helicopter pad on top of a building in *Mad City*. He wonders where this helicopter could take him. What would he notice as he flies high above the neighborhood? He's pretty sure he's spotted a secret hideout located on the side of the mountain.

Jade is using her earnings from working at the pizza place to buy new furniture for her bedroom. She doesn't want anything boring or ordinary for her room though. She wants furniture that has the ability to transport her to another time and place.

_____

_____

_____

_____

_____

_____

_____

_____

_____

_____

_____

_____

_____

_____

_____

_____

_____

Sutton is a dancer in the *Royal Academy Ballet* of *Roblox*. She wishes she could be a prestigious ballet dancer in real life, but she lives far away from the nearest dance studio. How can she become a famous ballerina while she's stuck in this town?

_____

_____

_____

_____

_____

_____

_____

_____

_____

_____

_____

_____

_____

_____

_____

_____

Alex needs money to complete her house in *Welcome to Bloxburg*, so she decides to get a job. She notices a job opening as a woodcutter. She knows what kind of creations she could make as a woodcutter, but she laughs to herself when she decides where she wants to display them.

Michael noticed no one was coming to his house in Bloxburg. As a matter of fact, he was completely alone in his big house. He knew this house had secrets and that one day, the secrets would be revealed.

_____

_____

_____

_____

_____

_____

_____

_____

_____

_____

_____

_____

_____

_____

_____

_____

Julie has never missed a day of school at *Robloxian High*—that is, until everything changed on her way to class one day.

_____

_____

_____

_____

_____

_____

_____

_____

_____

_____

_____

_____

_____

_____

_____

_____

_____

In this town, you can create your own amazing vehicle to drive from house to house. Sam wants to create the most unbelievable vehicle, one the world has never seen before. It will have one feature that will make everyone's jaw drop.

_____

_____

_____

_____

_____

_____

_____

_____

_____

_____

_____

_____

_____

_____

_____

The house Emily is building will be legendary. The best part is the room with the hidden secret that only her closest friends and family members can access. When they see this room, their minds will be blown.

_____

_____

_____

_____

_____

_____

_____

_____

_____

_____

_____

_____

_____

_____

_____

_____

_____

Jamie is working hard to finish building her estate. But every time she goes to her new mansion, she notices changes that she didn't make. Who would go into her home and change things around? And, more importantly, why would they want to?

It's time for Cadyn to go to work at the best pizza place in town. Today, he's invented a new pizza recipe no one has ever tried. He wonders if his boss will like the idea and let him add it to the menu.

_____

_____

_____

_____

_____

_____

_____

_____

_____

_____

_____

_____

_____

_____

_____

_____

CHAPTER 3

BUILDING

Look around within *Roblox* and you'll quickly see all the building taking place. Whether it's a skyscraper or a scary roller coaster, it takes a big imagination and a lot of work to keep constructing these extraordinary places.

Zion wants to build his own theme park, the way you can in *Theme Park Tycoon 2*. But his parents won't let him ride roller coasters, so he doesn't know what it's like to be a passenger on this ride.

_____

_____

_____

_____

_____

_____

_____

_____

_____

_____

_____

_____

_____

_____

_____

Cameron dreams of living in a huge skyscraper one day. This skyscraper would be filled with surprises and adventures around every corner—not like the boring office buildings you see downtown.

_____

_____

_____

_____

_____

_____

_____

_____

_____

_____

_____

_____

_____

_____

_____

Time to build your own island. This island will be special, with hidden items you must forage so you can survive. You've found a few useful items, but this latest find has to be the absolute best.

_____

_____

_____

_____

_____

_____

_____

_____

_____

_____

_____

_____

_____

_____

_____

_____

_____

Jack always thought Evan was one of his best friends. But every time Jack creates a new game about building, Evan makes fun of it and refuses to play. Jack wishes Evan would support him and is puzzled by his friend's actions.

Malcolm is building a restaurant, and he's working hard to make it world-famous. He must use powerful cooking appliances and hire the best waiters and waitresses. What else can he do to make it legendary?

_____

_____

_____

_____

_____

_____

_____

_____

_____

_____

_____

_____

_____

_____

_____

Tamira daydreams of designing the most exciting new video game the world has ever experienced. She plans to include features that no player has ever laid eyes on. Just wait until her friends see how she designs the buildings and cities in her new game.

_____

_____

_____

_____

_____

_____

_____

_____

_____

_____

_____

_____

_____

_____

_____

_____

Lauren has ideas about how to build her dream car. This car will be mind-blowing, complete with invisible doors and the ability to fly. Everyone will be so jealous when she starts driving it to school every day.

_____

_____

_____

_____

_____

_____

_____

_____

_____

_____

_____

_____

_____

_____

_____

_____

_____

The roller-coaster ride has more loops and turns than anyone thought possible. The best part is when it disappears into thin air—and then reappears. Where the roller coaster disappears to is a complete mystery. Why would anyone ever build a roller coaster like this?

Violet would like to build her own house, one that's full of windows so she can easily see all the creatures passing by each day. She wonders what would happen if the creatures peered into her windows or what they would think of the house she built.

The hotel looks grand from the outside. But on the inside each floor is either good or evil. No one knows what a hotel floor will be like until they step off the elevator. Then reality sets in.

Isabel is ready to build her company from the ground up. She has big plans to create a business unlike anyone else's. Some people think her ideas will never work, but others think her business ideas are pure genius.

_____

_____

_____

_____

_____

_____

_____

_____

_____

_____

_____

_____

_____

_____

_____

_____

Luis wants to be his own boss and start a company where he will hire only the robots he built. These robots will take care of all the important daily tasks, such as collecting mail. Then there will be other robots that perform tasks no one has ever seen before.

_____

_____

_____

_____

_____

_____

_____

_____

_____

_____

_____

_____

_____

_____

Avery wants to build an award-winning restaurant and serve only the best food. She dreams of becoming the richest chef in the world. She knows exactly what she would spend her first paycheck on.

_____

_____

_____

_____

_____

_____

_____

_____

_____

_____

_____

_____

_____

_____

_____

CHAPTER 4

ROLE PLAY

Role play means you can become any character your mind can dream of in any location you can imagine. *Roblox* offers us many opportunities to take on a new personality or live in a new world.

Jessica is ready to put on her gear to fight the monsters, just like in *RPG Simulator*. She has a companion who helps her fight evil—but today her companion hasn't shown up.

_____

_____

_____

_____

_____

_____

_____

_____

_____

_____

_____

_____

_____

_____

_____

_____

Henry likes to play on Earth while he works his way through *Royale High*. It makes him think about living on another planet besides Earth. He's curious about how different life in a new world would be and what it would take to survive there every day.

_____

_____

_____

_____

_____

_____

_____

_____

_____

_____

_____

_____

_____

_____

_____

_____

_____

Dante finds this island so interesting to explore. It's complete with its own vegetation and lots of tropical fruits. Everything seems wonderful—until he meets the islanders and sees what's in their houses.

_____

_____

_____

_____

_____

_____

_____

_____

_____

_____

_____

_____

_____

_____

_____

Bailey wonders what her pet does all day. She wonders how much time she spends eating, sleeping, and wandering around. Bailey also notices that her pet disappears for a while. Perhaps her pet has a whole other identity that Bailey doesn't even know about.

_____

_____

_____

_____

_____

_____

_____

_____

_____

_____

_____

_____

_____

_____

_____

_____

Lucy's pet unicorn can fly into the most interesting places. It's amazing where this unicorn has been and what she has seen. Lucy wishes she could join her pet on one of her adventures. They would have so much fun together.

This potion will make Luciano's pet able to fly. Luciano wonders what would happen if he himself drank the potion. Could he fly alongside his pet? How else would his life change?

Josie is trying to age her pet so it will hurry up and be fully grown. This makes her curious about what it would be like to age her own self. She could skip ahead and finally get to her favorite age in life. What would she be like?

_____

_____

_____

_____

_____

_____

_____

_____

_____

_____

_____

_____

_____

_____

_____

_____

Penelope and Abby did everything together and were the best of friends—until one day when Abby thought Penelope scammed her in the game. She even took Abby's favorite pet. But was this really Penelope, or was it an impostor?

_____

_____

_____

_____

_____

_____

_____

_____

_____

_____

_____

_____

_____

_____

_____

_____

_____

Carlos is ready to show everyone how he can use his saber to defeat the bad guys. But to use it correctly, he must first gather his strength. It's time for him to summon his own power and show his friends how strong he really is.

It's the Wild West, and Eva is a cowgirl ready to explore the land. Along the desert trails, she runs into plenty of strangers—and has strange encounters. What's going on out in the West?

Benjamin is exploring the island and notices something very unusual right away. If you live on the island, you're allowed to design your very own family any way you want. Benjamin has lots of ideas about what his family would be like.

Macy's amazing pet is the cutest pet ever, and it also has extraordinary abilities. Macy can't wait until her friends see what this pet can do.

_____

_____

_____

_____

_____

_____

_____

_____

_____

_____

_____

_____

_____

_____

_____

CHAPTER 5

COMEDY

We all need a little humor in our lives. Fortunately, we can find lots of funny experiences throughout our favorite video game.

Josephine wants to play *Make a Cake*. It's time to create a cake made from the yuckiest ingredients ever imagined. This cake is going to be epic.

It's time for Taylor to level up in this game, but first she has to read the map for clues. Some of these clues don't make any sense at all. What do a rotten banana and a pair of clown shoes even mean? She wonders where this map is going to lead her.

James is concerned because zombies are coming from everywhere. Every time he turns around, he sees a new one that's even uglier than the one before! James and his friends will have to devise a quick plan to get rid of them once and for all.

Hannah has worked tirelessly to get through the levels to escape the dungeon and slay the monster. She knows she needs more equipment to finally break free. Problem is, she found out the monster responds only to being held like a little baby. How is this going to work?

There's a restaurant that serves only the best food, uses the best appliances in the best kitchen, and has the best staff. Who gets to eat at this restaurant? Only pirates. But it won't be too long before the pirates take over the place.

_____

_____

_____

_____

_____

_____

_____

_____

_____

_____

_____

_____

_____

_____

_____

_____

_____

Remy can't stop laughing at his friend's username. It's possibly the silliest name he's ever heard. But when he asks his friend where it came from, Remy is shocked.

Mila loves marbles, so much so that she invented a game where she is stuck inside one and rolls around all through town. She has loads of fun until the day her marble takes on a life of its own.

_____

_____

_____

_____

_____

_____

_____

_____

_____

_____

_____

_____

_____

_____

_____

Elijah loves the thought of cloning himself. He would create crazy chaos if there were two of him. Oh wait, imagine the trouble it would cause if there were *five* of him running around!

This day care looks a little suspicious to Carrie. Does anyone else notice how strange the teacher is? What exactly does she do when she's not at work at the day care? Carrie is certain the teacher may not be human after all and has slime instead of blood running through her veins.

It's another bizarre day when nothing makes sense. It's hilarious to see how people function when everything is backward. The sky is down; the ground is up. Life will never be the same again.

As Ethan plays *Make a Cake*, he notices a lot of funny things taking place in a sewer. Turns out, the sewer is like a whole other world. Where do all the pipes lead to? Why would anyone want to live down there?

_____

_____

_____

_____

_____

_____

_____

_____

_____

_____

_____

_____

_____

_____

_____

_____

Isla's favorite restaurant has a giant candy machine. She imagines what it would be like to live inside the candy machine and have access to as many sweets as she wants. Her plan to live there sounds fantastic—until she realizes there's one big problem: all the candy is brain-flavored.

CHAPTER 6

HORROR

Who says horror is only for the movies? The horror games in *Roblox* provide loads of frightful fun for the player. Your stories will scare the daylights out of your readers with the help of these prompts.

Chloe is trying to escape in *Piggy* but can't find any keycards to unlock the doors. She switches her strategy and looks for a new skin, which will give her new supplies to help her escape. Since she can't get out with a keycard, she will have to reinvent her character. Whom will she become?

Frank wants to defeat the evil tycoon, just like in *Horror Tycoon*. But what did this tycoon ever do to Frank? What makes the tycoon so evil? What would make the tycoon a good person again?

_____

_____

_____

_____

_____

_____

_____

_____

_____

_____

_____

_____

_____

_____

_____

_____

Anders is trapped in a day care with five other friends. The teacher is a complete nightmare. Anders is convinced the teacher must be from another planet. But wait! He now has evidence she really is from another planet.

_____

_____

_____

_____

_____

_____

_____

_____

_____

_____

_____

_____

_____

_____

_____

_____

_____

The worst possible ending just happened during Jamie's mission as a soldier. How will he ever get out of this situation? Worse yet, there are only a few items from his airplane he can take with him to survive.

_____

_____

_____

_____

_____

_____

_____

_____

_____

_____

_____

_____

_____

_____

_____

_____

Leah must run away from the murderer. She has two choices: run into the woods or run into the town full of scary clowns. Each choice has a consequence. Which path should Leah take and why?

_____

_____

_____

_____

_____

_____

_____

_____

_____

_____

_____

_____

_____

_____

_____

The murderer left a trail of clues behind, and Jonah is the only one who can find them. Each of these clues has a special meaning that will lead Jonah to find more. But what are these clues, and why did the murderer want only Jonah to find them?

A mystery surrounds this beast, and no one can figure it out. There must be a way to escape from the beast—or else defeat it—once and for all. Noah must quickly devise a plan to get rid of it so everyone will be safe.

_____

_____

_____

_____

_____

_____

_____

_____

_____

_____

_____

_____

_____

_____

_____

_____

_____

The killer banana cannot be stopped. It keeps chasing Isaiah everywhere he goes. Maybe if he goes through this maze, then he'll lose the banana. Ugh, why is this maze so hard, and where is the strange smell coming from?

_____

_____

_____

_____

_____

_____

_____

_____

_____

_____

_____

_____

_____

_____

_____

_____

Hamilton was on his way to day care and ready to play with all his friends. But once he got there, he quickly realized all his friends and teachers had been replaced with...

_____

_____

_____

_____

_____

_____

_____

_____

_____

_____

_____

_____

_____

_____

Rebecca is trapped in the dungeon, and she must overcome the obstacles to escape from the wicked king. She has twenty obstacles to overcome, and each one is harder than the last. Will she make it out alive?

_____

_____

_____

_____

_____

_____

_____

_____

_____

_____

_____

_____

_____

_____

_____

_____

_____

_____

The killer mouse is on the loose, and Daniel isn't so sure he'll come out of this unharmed. But this unusual "killer" can be stopped only with unusual methods. Daniel will have to do what has never been done before.

_____

_____

_____

_____

_____

_____

_____

_____

_____

_____

_____

_____

_____

_____

_____

_____

The only thing standing between Rosa and the zombies is a fortress she built. The zombies are headed straight toward her. She's hoping all the unique features she added to her fortress will be enough to protect her.

Mateo is trying to solve a murder mystery, but soon he realizes no one he's working with wants him to solve the case. He wonders why he's the only one who can solve the mystery, and why no one else wants to help.

CHAPTER 7

ANIMALS AND PETS

Animals and pets provide video games—and humans—plenty to talk about. Some animals are sweet and affectionate. Others are little monsters in disguise. What kind of creature will show up in your story?

Pet Show Dress Up is ready to showcase the style of Nahla's favorite animal—a cat. But Nahla realizes the cat isn't as cute or cuddly as the other animals. As a matter of fact, the cat seems downright scary.

_____

_____

_____

_____

_____

_____

_____

_____

_____

_____

_____

_____

_____

_____

_____

Tristan thinks it would be cool to live among a pack of wolves, the way he and his friends do in the game *Wolves' Life*. His pack would have a leader, and the other wolves would have their own unique roles. But one day one wolf decides to break off from the pack.

Carla is ready to study the sharks and get up close and personal with them. She wonders if this shark cage is sturdy enough to hold her and defend her against the sharks. It sure looks a little flimsy.

Niki's character is the shortfin mako shark. This shark is known for being incredibly fast and a great hunter. Not only can it quickly get anywhere in the ocean, but it can also even jump out of the water. Niki would love to have these same powers.

Xavier thinks his pet bird wants to leave its nest and join a new flock. But what makes a new flock so special? Why doesn't his bird like his nest now?

_____

_____

_____

_____

_____

_____

_____

_____

_____

_____

_____

_____

_____

_____

_____

Bella dreams of owning her own pet Pegasus. After all, they are such magical and mythical creatures. She can think of plenty of places where her Pegasus could take her. Their adventures together would be endless.

_____

_____

_____

_____

_____

_____

_____

_____

_____

_____

_____

_____

_____

_____

Hunter wants a pet pig so badly, but his parents refuse to let him have one. He devises a plan to keep a pet pig at his secret hideaway. The best part? His parents will never find out.

_____

_____

_____

_____

_____

_____

_____

_____

_____

_____

_____

_____

_____

_____

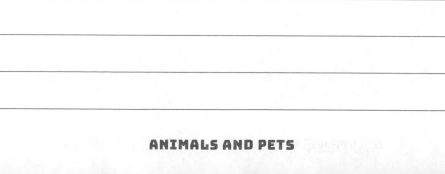
The teacher asked Anna what her favorite pet would be. Everyone in class laughed at Anna when she told them she would choose a pet unicorn that could fly while she rode on its back. But why is that so funny? It could happen—with a little magic.

_____

_____

_____

_____

_____

_____

_____

_____

_____

_____

_____

_____

_____

_____

_____

David noticed for a while that his pet cats were acting strange. It was almost as if the cats were working behind his back and plotting something against him. Then, one day, the cats' secret plans finally came to life.

✏ Martina knows that if she's going to live in the Wild West, she must have a trusty horse as a companion. Imagine all the places the horse would take her. Imagine how Martina would feel if one day her horse got lost and she couldn't find it.

_____

_____

_____

_____

_____

_____

_____

_____

_____

_____

_____

_____

_____

_____

_____

_____

The pet show is about to begin and the star of the show—Piggy—is nowhere to be found. Where could she be? The last place she was seen was on top of the building. What was she doing up there, and what is she plotting?

_____

_____

_____

_____

_____

_____

_____

_____

_____

_____

_____

_____

_____

_____

_____

Marlowe wants a new pet, one that follows her everywhere she goes and loves her unconditionally. The only problem? Her mom won't let her have one because she doesn't like animals. Marlowe creates a plan to get a pet and ensure her mom will never find out.

The swarm of bees is so interesting. Each bee has its own distinct personality and contributes in its own way to the colony. But they all work together and serve their queen while building the colony. What goes on inside the world of these bees?

CHAPTER 8

AN ASSORTMENT OF TOPICS

Roblox is like life: you never know which direction the story will take. Here's an assortment of topics, based on several different games within *Roblox*, that can take your story to soaring new heights.

Emma loves to play the piano in *Roblox's Got Talent*. The judges consistently award her with the first-place honor. She's never played the piano in real life, but it's fun having a secret talent that her parents aren't even aware she has.

Jackson desperately wants a new skin for his character, but it will cost 300 Robux. He doesn't have any Robux or his own money to purchase more for his skin. He must figure out a way to earn additional money—and fast.

Caroline came in last place in *Fashion Famous*. She was confused because her outfit was much more creative than the other contestants' outfits. She's frustrated because she spent a lot of time and Robux to create something unique.

_____

_____

_____

_____

_____

_____

_____

_____

_____

_____

_____

_____

_____

_____

_____

_____

_____

_____

Shevon has reached a portal in *Islands* that will take him to a new farm to forage. This place is full of interesting characters and secret places designed to help Shevon build the ultimate island for sole survival.

Looks like an intense dance competition is taking place on a level in *The Normal Elevator*. Jasmine dreams of dancing on a stage one day. The only problem is, she's never taken a dance lesson in her life, and none of her friends know how to dance. How will she learn?

Kristen is playing the *Sole Survivor* game with her friend Lily, when Lily says she wants to play a different game. But Kristen has collected almost all of her needed supplies and doesn't want to quit. Lily says she is ignoring her, and they get into an argument. What can they do to solve this?

Hudson notices a scene with a beach in a game he is playing. It reminds him of what happened to him and his family last summer on vacation...

_____

_____

_____

_____

_____

_____

_____

_____

_____

_____

_____

_____

_____

_____

_____

_____

_____

_____

The golden knife is nowhere to be found, and Brianna is the one player who can help get the knife. There must be a way to get the truth out of her, but what will it take for her to talk?

_____

_____

_____

_____

_____

_____

_____

_____

_____

_____

_____

_____

_____

_____

_____

_____

_____

Max dreams of winning the award for best video game one day. He knows his creation is the most imaginative one ever played. No other game looks like his—until Stevie tries to copy it.

_____

_____

_____

_____

_____

_____

_____

_____

_____

_____

_____

_____

_____

_____

_____

_____

_____

Lizzy thinks it's rude that her so-called friend Haley won't let her play a game in Haley's private server. What did Lizzy do to make Haley shut her out? Can Lizzy and Haley remain friends?

_____

_____

_____

_____

_____

_____

_____

_____

_____

_____

_____

_____

_____

_____

_____

_____

_____

It's time for Charlotte to plan her digital dream wedding. This wedding will be so fabulous that everyone will copy it. The wedding is complete with the cutest pets, flowers, and cake. If only she could get rid of this obby though.

Darius must sell his most prized possession for coins so he can finish building his island. He's not sure he can do it though. After all, this special thing has been with him for so long. He remembers when he got it like it was yesterday. It's such a funny story.

Kayla will do anything to win a Bloxy award—including stealing a game idea from her friend Katy. But when Katy finds out, Kayla had better watch out. Katy has a few tricks up her sleeve too.

_____

_____

_____

_____

_____

_____

_____

_____

_____

_____

_____

_____

_____

_____

_____

_____

BLANK
JOURNAL PAGES

✏

101 UNOFFICIAL ROBLOX STORY STARTERS

ABOUT THE AUTHOR

Sara Coleman is a former corporate gal turned creative entrepreneur. She began writing professionally several years ago and now contributes to multiple websites, blogs, and magazines. She's also an avid reader and can't resist a great historical fiction book. Sara holds a BA in journalism from the University of Georgia and can be found supporting her Bulldogs every chance she has. She resides in Charlotte, North Carolina, with her wonderfully supportive husband and three children. When she's not ushering her kids to sports and dance lessons, she can be found creating content for her own website, TheProperPen.com.